MOVIE MAGIC
COSTUMES
AND PROPS

BY SARA GREEN

BELLWETHER MEDIA • MINNEAPOLIS, MN

Blastoff! Discovery launches a new mission: reading to learn. Filled with facts and features, each book offers you an exciting new world to explore!

This edition first published in 2019 by Bellwether Media, Inc.

Library of Congress Cataloging-in-Publication Data

Names: Green, Sara, 1964- author.
Title: Costumes and Props / by Sara Green.
Description: First edition. | Minneapolis, MN : Bellwether Media, Inc., 2019. | Series: Blastoff! Discovery: Movie Magic | Includes bibliographical references and index.
Identifiers: LCCN 2018005001 (print) | LCCN 2018016194 (ebook) | ISBN 9781681035888 (ebook) | ISBN 9781626178472 (hardcover : alk. paper)
Subjects: LCSH: Clothing and dress in motion pictures–Juvenile literature.
Classification: LCC PN1995.9.C56 (ebook) | LCC PN1995.9.C56 G74 2019 (print) | DDC 791.4302/6–dc23
LC record available at https://lccn.loc.gov/2018005001

Editor: Betsy Rathburn   Designer: Brittany McIntosh

Printed in the United States of America, North Mankato, MN.

TABLE OF CONTENTS

THE ACTION BEGINS

Time to suit up! The Avengers must prepare to fight. Tony Stark changes into his Iron Man suit. Captain America grabs his red, white, and blue shield. Thor raises a large hammer to the sky. Hawkeye readies his bow and arrow.

The characters will use their suits and weapons in a battle to save the earth!

IRON MAN

CAPTAIN AMERICA

Behind the camera, a **crew** works hard to make sure the costumes and props are right for each **scene**. Costume designer Alexandra Byrne leads a team of more than 60 people. Together, they make sure the superhero costumes fit the actors!

There is a props crew, too. **Props master** Andrew Petrotta makes sure the weapons look good. He makes sure the background looks realistic. Props and costumes bring the movie to life!

FOODIES

Props masters are often responsible for food that actors eat on camera. Mashed bananas are often used as ice cream. Bread can be cut to look like meat!

WHAT ARE COSTUMES AND PROPS?

Actors wear costumes to play characters. Costume designers choose and design the outfits based on the movie's story. Costumes reveal information about the characters. They can show how rich a character is or what time period they live in.

One example is Jack Sparrow in *Pirates of the Caribbean*. His clothes are as sloppy as he is! Other characters in the movie wear clothing that looks dated. This shows the movie takes place at a different point in history.

BEST DRESSED

The character Rose in the 1997 film *Titanic* boards the ship wearing a stylish white dress and a lavender hat with a wide brim. These clothes show that Rose is wealthy.

CAPTAIN
JACK SPARROW

The lightsabers used in the
Star Wars movies are hero props.

STAR WARS:
THE FORCE AWAKENS

Props are objects used by actors in a film. Like costumes, props help tell the story of a movie. Almost anything can be a prop. Hero props are items used by the main actors. These props are often filmed up close.

Other props are made especially for **stunts**. For example, some movies use chairs that break easily without hurting anyone. Furniture and other large items are called **set** props. Background props lack details because they are rarely seen close up.

HERO PROP FROM
THE LORD OF THE RINGS:
THE RETURN OF THE KING

EARLY COSTUMES AND PROPS

In the early years of motion pictures, actors often created their own costumes. Sometimes, they wore clothes from their own closets! That changed in 1916. Filmmaker D.W. Griffith hired a woman named Clare West to design costumes. Audiences loved West's work. She inspired other filmmakers to use costume designers.

Another famous designer of the time was a man named Gilbert Adrian. He designed beautiful costumes for a 1938 film called *Marie Antoinette*. One gown weighed 108 pounds (49 kilograms)!

OUTFITTING OZ

Gilbert Adrian designed the costumes for the 1939 movie *The Wizard of Oz*. One pair of Dorothy's ruby slippers is on display at the National Museum of American History in Washington, D.C.

COSTUME DESIGN PIONEER

Name: Edith Head

Born: October 28, 1897, in San Bernardino, California

Famous For: Costume designer who became the first female head designer at any major studio in 1938 and designed costumes for famous movies like *All About Eve* (1950) and *Roman Holiday* (1953)

Awards: 8 Academy Awards for Costume Design, the most Academy Awards won by a woman

ROMAN HOLIDAY

HARRISON FORD
AS INDIANA JONES

Some film costumes started fashion trends. For example, the 1951 film *A Streetcar Named Desire* led to a spike in T-shirt sales. Actor Marlon Brando famously wore one in the movie.

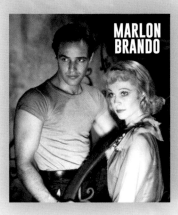

MARLON BRANDO

Many other characters have worn memorable outfits. Indiana Jones, played by actor Harrison Ford, wore a **fedora** in the Indiana Jones film series. Harrison Ford also played Han Solo in the Star Wars film series. His costume included a black vest and **holster**.

A FEARSOME LOOK

John Mollo worked from drawings by artist Ralph McQuarrie to design Darth Vader's helmet for the Star Wars film series. It was made to look like helmets worn by Japanese warriors!

Props also help create a film's look and story. But they are not always what they seem. Early filmmakers learned to be creative when making props for their movies. For example, Charlie Chaplin's character eats a boot in the 1925 film *The Gold Rush*. It looks real, but the boot is really made of licorice!

Later movies continued using unusual materials for props. The 1939 movie *The Wizard of Oz* featured an hourglass filled with what looked like red sand. But the real sand could not be dyed at that time. It was really strawberry Jell-O!

HOURGLASS FROM *THE WIZARD OF OZ*

THE GOLD RUSH

WILLY WONKA
& THE CHOCOLATE FACTORY

Some early props were very simple. The 1956 film *The Red Balloon* featured a shiny balloon that followed a boy around. As movie cameras became more advanced, more detailed props were needed. The golden ticket in the 1971 movie *Willy Wonka & the Chocolate Factory* was made of gold foil with black letters. This helped it stand out on camera!

Other movies needed items that do not exist in real life. Props masters had to be creative. For example, the original lightsabers in the Star Wars series were made from camera parts. The communicator in the 1982 movie *E.T. the Extra-Terrestrial* was made from everyday objects like toys and an umbrella!

MAKING MIDDLE EARTH

Thousands of props were made for the Lord of the Rings films. They included about 1,000 suits of armor and 2,000 hobbit feet for the four main hobbits!

FAVORITE FILMS
COME ALIVE!

Over time, costumes and props have continued to delight movie audiences. The Harry Potter film series featured outstanding examples of both. Costume designer Jany Temime worked on several Harry Potter films. Her original designs included Hermione's pink ball gown and Luna's Christmas tree dress.

Memorable props in the series make Harry's world a reality. These include wands, potions, and Quidditch broomsticks. More than 200,000 coins were made for the Gringotts scene in *Harry Potter and the Deathly Hallows: Part 2*!

WEARY WANDS

Daniel Radcliffe, the actor who played Harry Potter, wore out more than 60 wands while filming the series.

The Hunger Games film series also featured impressive props and costumes. Costume designers created many outfits for Katniss Everdeen. They included drab clothes and stunning gowns. These costumes helped show how Katniss changed over time.

Props also added excitement to the films. Audiences feared for Katniss and Peeta when they almost ate deadly nightlock berries. But they were really blueberries! Katniss's mockingjay pin was specially made for the film. It reminded audiences of her rebellion!

EXTRA WORK

The costume designers for the movie *The Hunger Games: Catching Fire* designed 5,800 costumes for the extras to wear.

THE HUNGER GAMES

Sometimes, animated movies are recreated with real actors. Costume designers are challenged to bring cartoon costumes to life. The 2015 movie *Cinderella* made the character's famous blue gown a reality. The dress was made with more than 10,000 crystals!

Colorful costumes in the 2017 film *Beauty and the Beast* helped make a magical world become real. Belle's yellow dress was designed so actress Emma Watson could move and dance in it. Both movies were **nominated** for **Academy Awards** for Costume Design!

CINDERELLA

MORE SPARKLES

About 20,000 crystals were used to make a coat for the prince in *Beauty and the Beast*.

THOR

Props can help audiences learn about characters and their stories. In the Marvel film *Guardians of the Galaxy*, Peter Quill carries a Walkman. This tells the audience that he likes music! It also shows that he lived in the 1980s when the music player was popular.

PETER QUILL

Some Marvel props presented challenges. Thor's powerful hammer needed to look heavy in the movie. But the actor needed to lift it easily. The props master made the hammer out of rubber!

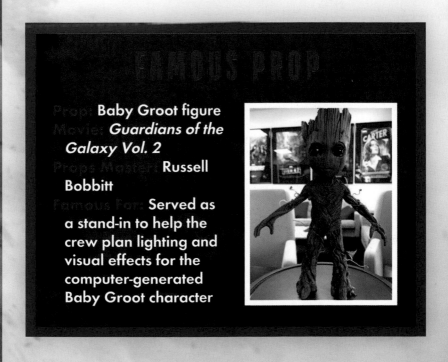

FAMOUS PROP

Prop: **Baby Groot figure**
Movie: ***Guardians of the Galaxy Vol. 2***
Props Master: **Russell Bobbitt**
Famous For: **Served as a stand-in to help the crew plan lighting and visual effects for the computer-generated Baby Groot character**

THE FUTURE OF
COSTUMES AND PROPS

Traditionally, film crews created costumes and props by hand. They also shopped for what they needed. Today, other methods make costume and prop design easier and faster.

One growing design method is **3D printing**. Designers create computer models of items needed for a film. Then, a 3D printer makes them! Many of the props in *Star Wars: The Force Awakens* were created this way. Costumes and props will always play an important role in movies. They help stories come to life on the big screen!

FAMOUS COSTUME DESIGNER

Name: Michael Kaplan
Born: Philadelphia, Pennsylvania
Famous For: Costume designer who created many costumes for the Star Wars film series, including some Stormtrooper uniforms and Kylo Ren's cloak
Awards: 1983 BAFTA for Best Costume Design in the film *Blade Runner*

KYLO REN IN
STAR WARS: THE FORCE AWAKENS

GLOSSARY

3D printing—the process of making an object in which models are scanned and printed using many thin layers of materials stacked on top of one another

Academy Awards—yearly awards presented for achievement in film; an Academy Award is also called an Oscar.

crew—a group of people who use special technical and practical skills to help make a movie

fedora—a hat with a soft brim and an indented crown

holster—a case for holding a firearm on the body

nominated—to be chosen as a candidate for an award

props master—the person in charge of the props in a movie

scene—the action in a single place and time in a film or play

set—the place where a movie is made

stunts—dangerous or risky acts in a movie

TO LEARN MORE

AT THE LIBRARY

Hammelef, Danielle S. *Behind-the-Scenes Movie Careers*. North Mankato, Minn.: Capstone Press, 2017.

Horn, Geoffrey M. *Movie Makeup, Costumes, and Sets*. Milwaukee, Wis.: G. Stevens Pub., 2007.

Quijano, Jonathan. *Make Your Own Sci-Fi Flick*. Mankato, Minn.: Capstone Press, 2012.

ON THE WEB

Learning more about costumes and props is as easy as 1, 2, 3.

1. Go to www.factsurfer.com.

2. Enter "costumes and props" into the search box.

3. Click the "Surf" button and you will see a list of related web sites.

With factsurfer.com, finding more information is just a click away.

INDEX

The images in this book are reproduced through the courtesy of: Moviestore collection Ltd/ Alamy, front cover, pp. 3, 12, 24-25; Collection Christophel/ Alamy, p. 4; Photo 12/ Alamy, pp. 4-5, 8; Walt Disney Studios Motion Pictures/ Photofest Digital, pp. 6-7; Stephen Barnes/ Entertainment/ Alamy, p. 7; AF Archive/ Alamy, pp. 9, 10-11, 15 (top), 19, 26-27; New Line/ Everett Collection, p. 11; ZUMA Press, Inc/ Alamy, p. 13 (top); Everett Collection, p. 13 (bottom); Atlaspix/ Alamy, p. 14; Polaris/ Newscom, p. 15 (bottom); Associated Press/ AP Images, p. 16; ClassicStock/Alamy, pp. 16-17; Entertainment Pictures/ Alamy, pp. 18-19; Brittany McIntosh, p. 20; Warner Brothers/ Everett Collection, pp. 20-21; Lionsgate/ Everett Collection, pp. 22, 22-23; Walt Disney Studios Motion Pictures/ Everett Collection, pp. 24, 27 (top); Blaublau94/ Wikipedia, p. 27 (bottom); Sarunyu L, p. 28; Jamie McCarthy/ Getty Images, p. 29 (top); Walt Disney Studios Motion Pictures/ Lucasfilm Ltd./ Everett Collection, p. 29 (bottom).